THE LITTLE BOOK OF HAPPINESS

Summersdale Publishers Ltd
46 West Street
Chichester
West Sussex
PO19 1RP
UK

www.summersdale.com

Printed and bound in the Czech Republic

ISBN: 978-1-84953-790-2

Substantial discounts on bulk quantities of Summersdale books are available to corporations, professional associations and other organisations. For details contact Nicky Douglas by telephone: +44 (0) 1243 756902, fax: +44 (0) 1243 786300 or email: nicky@summersdale.com.

the little book of
HAPPINESS

lucy lane

INTRODUCTION

Life can be stressful, but sometimes we simply need to adjust our expectations and thought processes in order to achieve happiness. Whether it's sharing a joke with a friend, helping a stranger or taking a moment to stand still and enjoy the sensations of the world around us, happiness is always in our reach. This collection of inspiring suggestions and joyful quotations will set you on a cheerful path, so you can make the most of everything life has to offer!

SIMPLE PLEASURES ARE THE BEST

Savour the everyday things that you enjoy. Focus on anything you like – hugging your pet, drinking a refreshing juice or smelling the food you are about to eat. Give yourself time to notice these agreeable things and life becomes full of plentiful small pleasures.

Wealth consists not in
having great possessions,
but in having few wants.

Epictetus

Nothing really matters
except what you do now
in this instant of time.

Eileen Caddy

START THE DAY WELL

Begin each day with a positive morning routine. Allow yourself time for meditation (or at least a moment of reflection), a healthy breakfast and some exercise. You can then move into your day calm and happy.

Don't cry because it's over, **smile** because it **happened**.

Dr Seuss

True happiness is an inner power – natural, healing, abundant and always available.

Robert Holden

DON'T FORGET HOW GREAT YOU ARE!

Notice when self-criticism starts to ring around inside your head. Low levels of self-esteem correlate to lower feelings of happiness, so try to put things into perspective. Build up your sense of appreciation for the positive skills and attributes you possess and recognise the blessings around you in life.

Laughter is an
instant vacation.

Milton Berle

With the new day
comes new strength
and new thoughts.

Eleanor Roosevelt

CHANGE YOUR LANGUAGE

Change your words and you will change your feelings. Replace 'I have to do it' with 'I want to do it'. This creates an energetic shift and enables you to feel more empowered. Try it any time you hear yourself thinking 'I have to' or 'I should'. Also, try saying YES more – it might just change your life!

HAPPINESS DEPENDS UPON OURSELVES.

Aristotle

Life isn't about finding yourself. Life is about creating yourself.

George Bernard Shaw

IT'S PLAYTIME!

Make time to play! It could be a game of rounders in the garden, a cricket match on the beach, an 'I spy' competition in the car or an evening of tiddlywinks by the fireside. Have good old-fashioned fun with friends and family, and enjoy smiles all round.

Wherever you are
– be all there.

Jim Elliot

Happiness comes
when your work and
words are of benefit to
yourself and others.

Jack Kornfield

LIVE THE LIFE YOU'VE DREAMED

Remember the dreams you had as a child to travel the world, work with horses or be an actor? If those dreams have not been fulfilled, visualise what passions still remain. How could you manifest a part of your dream into your current life? Perhaps book a trip abroad, go for a horse ride along the seashore or sign up with your local amateur dramatic society.

Dream **lofty** dreams, and as you dream, so you shall **become**.

James Allen

Success is getting what you want, happiness is wanting what you get.

W. P. Kinsella

THINK YOURSELF HAPPY

Your brain reacts in exactly the same way whether you are experiencing something that makes you feel happy or just thinking about something happy – both can flood your body with feel-good hormones. This means that you can influence how you feel by what you choose to think about. So think happy!

Change your thoughts
and you change
your world.

Norman Vincent Peale

If you carry joy in
your heart, you can
heal any moment.

Carlos Santana

GRATITUDE IS GREAT

Be appreciative of the things others do for you. Buddhist monks call this 'watering the flowers of gratitude'. Every week, sit down with someone you are close to and tell them all the things you have appreciated about them in the previous days. Let them do the same for you. Practised regularly, this can be a relationship changer.

ALL THE
HAPPINESS
THERE IS IN THIS
WORLD ARISES
FROM WISHING
OTHERS TO
BE HAPPY.

Geshe Kelsang Gyatso

Life is a shipwreck, but we must not forget to sing in the lifeboats.

Voltaire

PICK YOURSELF UP WHEN YOU FALL

The word 'resilience' stems from the Latin *resilio*, meaning 'to jump back'. In our everyday lives we need to find ways of bouncing back from adversity, to pick ourselves up and carry on. Having supportive friends around us and managing our behaviour positively are two helpful resilience strategies.

Mix a little foolishness
with your serious plans.
It is lovely to be silly
at the right moment.

Horace

Every time you smile at someone, it is an action of love, a gift to that person, a beautiful thing.

Mother Teresa

HAVE FUN TOGETHER

The happiest couples are those who spend time together doing enjoyable activities. However busy life becomes, make time to share fun – even if it's just exercising, browsing a farmers' market or watching a film. Staying in touch with and making time for friends is equally valuable.

Don't get your knickers in a knot. **Nothing** is solved and it just makes you walk **funny**.

Kathryn Carpenter

If you can solve your problem, then what is the need of worrying? If you cannot solve it, then what is the use of worrying?

Shantideva

FOLLOW YOUR PASSIONS

What are you passionate about? What energises you? Which of your friends do you have the most fun with? Recognise how you can choose to lift your spirits by following your heart. Always be true to yourself and what *you* love and enjoy.

Do what you can,
with what you have,
where you are.

Theodore Roosevelt

The greatest happiness
is to transform one's
feelings into action.

Madame de Staël

LET YOUR THOUGHTS BE THOUGHTS

Humans have over 60,000 thoughts a day. We can't change what we are feeling but we can alter our reactions to our thoughts. This means becoming conscious of what we are thinking, identifying the thought and realising that it need not dictate our lives. We can observe our thoughts and feelings, let them go and carry on.

**GO CONFIDENTLY
IN THE DIRECTION
OF YOUR DREAMS.
LIVE THE LIFE
YOU'VE IMAGINED.**

Henry David Thoreau

Begin to be now what
you will be hereafter.

William James

CREATE A HAPPINESS BOX

Whether it's a shoebox or your bedside drawer, this is your treasure chest, containing pieces of paper on which you have written some moments of happiness. Any time you experience something that has made you smile, filled you with joy or given you immense satisfaction – write it on some paper, fold it up and place in your box. You can then take them out and read through all your moments when you want to boost your happiness levels.

One joy scatters a hundred griefs.

Chinese proverb

Whenever you fall,
pick something up.

Oswald Avery

WALK ON THE WILD SIDE

Animals have been proven to be natural mood enhancers. By spending time with a pet you may see a reduction in your stress levels – and plenty of reasons to laugh and be cheerful! If you don't have a pet, why not pay a visit to a friend or relative who does.

Happiness is not a goal... it's a by-product of a life well lived.

Eleanor Roosevelt

Turn your face to the
sun and the shadows
fall behind you.

Maori proverb

BE HERE NOW

Santosa is a Sanskrit word meaning 'contentment and acceptance for where we are right now'. Allow this beautiful word to enter your vocabulary and let its message brighten your daily life. Bringing a little more *santosa* into your life will enable you to be fully present in the moment, and this will increase your overall sense of happiness.

Release your struggle, let go of your mind, throw away your concerns, and relax into the world.

Dan Millman

The only journey is
the one within.

Rainer Maria Rilke

I LIKE TO MOVE IT, MOVE IT

Our bodies produce chemicals called endorphins, which are natural happiness boosters. When you spend time doing something you truly enjoy, your body is flooded with these feel-good chemicals. So try to spend some time on joyful activities every day, from a quiet walk in the country or a park, to an exhilarating cycle ride or run.

A SMILE IS A CURVE THAT SETS EVERYTHING STRAIGHT.

Phyllis Diller

If you have good
thoughts they will shine
out of your face like
sunbeams and you will
always look lovely.

Roald Dahl

CELEBRATE YOUR GOALS

Be clear about what motivates you. High achievers have been found to have a strong desire to succeed, whereas those less accomplished simply wish to avoid failure. You can view demanding tasks as needing dedication and commitment, rather than as overloading and stressful. It's your choice!

Live today for tomorrow
it will all be history.

Proverb

Happiness is not
something ready-made.
It comes from your
own actions.

Dalai Lama

THE BRIGHT STUFF

Do you have a rainbow of coloured clothes in your wardrobe? Possibly not, but a brightly coloured item of clothing can help you show the world you are happy and full of beans. If you don't have any colourful clothes, make an effort to acquire some!

Keep smiling, because life is a **beautiful** thing and there's so much to **smile** about.

Marilyn Monroe

Look on every exit
as being an entrance
somewhere else.

Tom Stoppard

ALLOW YOURSELF TO LAUGH

Let go of heaviness – things don't have to be serious all the time. Lighten up with a joke and try to laugh at life's absurdities. Just be aware that true happiness comes from laughing *with* people, and not *at* them.

Life is either a daring
adventure or nothing.

Helen Keller

First say to yourself
what you would be;
and then do what
you have to do.

GET CREATIVE

Tap into your creativity. Reimagine an area of your living space or simply decorate or add some new touches to a room in your home; take up a brand new hobby such as watercolour painting, cake decorating or renovating old furniture – anything you feel comfortable with.

THERE ARE ALWAYS FLOWERS FOR THOSE WHO WANT TO SEE THEM.

Henri Matisse

Speak or act with a pure
mind and happiness
will follow you as your
shadow, unshakeable.

Buddha

What makes the
desert beautiful...
is that somewhere
it hides a well.

Antoine de Saint-Exupéry

MAKE TIME FOR THE THINGS THAT MATTER

The busier we get, the more we put other aspects of our lives on hold. An important contribution to our happiness is the time we spend with close family and good friends, so make the effort and plan a get-together, even if it's just a catch-up cup of tea.

Happiness arises in a state of peace, not a state of tumult.

Ann Radcliffe

You're the blacksmith
of your own happiness.

Swedish proverb

COME FLY WITH ME

Sit down and plan a trip to a destination you have dreamed of. Even if it may not happen for years, or not at all, it is uplifting and exciting to while away a few hours. Who knows, the dream may eventually become a reality!

Some days there won't
be a song in your
heart. Sing anyway.

Emory Austin

To be without some
of the things you want
is an indispensable
part of happiness.

Bertrand Russell

DEAL WITH WHAT'S WORRYING YOU

Sometimes chores remain in the back of our minds, waiting to get done. It could be checking out prices of electricity suppliers, renewing a magazine subscription or making an overdue dental appointment. For an instant happiness rush, deal with it now.

FALL SEVEN TIMES, STAND UP EIGHT.

Japanese proverb

For myself, I am an optimist – it does not seem to be much use being anything else.

Winston Churchill

LISTEN TO ALL YOUR SENSES

Slow down and pay attention to your surroundings. Use all your senses to enjoy your current environment, and before moving on, get your next destination clear in your mind.

Once you replace negative thoughts with positive ones, you'll start having positive results.

Willie Nelson

Be in love with your
life, every detail of it.

Jack Kerouac

ENJOY DOING THINGS WELL

Find little things that you're good at and allow simplicity to give meaning and purpose to your life. You don't have to strive to be the world's greatest at anything in order to be happy – doing everything to the best of your ability is enough!

One may **walk** over the highest mountain one **step** at a time.

John Wanamaker

If you ask me what
I came into this life
to do, I will tell you:
I came to live out loud.

Émile Zola

LIVE IN A JOYFUL NETWORK

Research shows that our happiness not only flourishes with those in our direct social network, such as neighbours, friends and family, but is influenced by the people our friends know too. So joyfulness echoes out through groups of people, like a radar system. Keep in contact and spread the joy!

At the height of laughter,
the universe is flung
into a kaleidoscope
of new possibilities.

Jean Houston

Cheerfulness is the
very flower of health.

Proverb

TAKE STEPS TO HAPPINESS

Walking is one of the most effective ways to replenish your inner joy, so incorporate a short walk into your daily routine if you can. The more you walk, the more you'll see – and you'll soon find yourself looking forward to taking to the pavements, in all weathers!

FOLKS ARE USUALLY ABOUT AS HAPPY AS THEY MAKE UP THEIR MINDS TO BE.

Abraham Lincoln

Find ecstasy in life;
the mere sense of
living is joy enough.

Emily Dickinson

HAPPY SNACKING

Have you noticed that when you feel in a low mood you may have intense cravings for foods containing refined sugar, like chocolate and cake? This is your body's way of getting a quick fix of happiness, because eating sugar produces insulin which elicits a temporary feeling of elation. Better food choices to improve your mood would be those rich in vitamin B6, such as spinach and salmon, and magnesium-rich foods like bananas and oat bran.

You are never too old
to set another goal or
to dream a new dream.

C. S. Lewis

We are all in the gutter
but some of us are
looking at the stars.

Oscar Wilde

EXPERIENCE THE NATURAL WORLD

Sometimes we need to make time to be in awe of life. Stand on the top of a mountain or hill, or look up at an expanse of night sky in the wilderness. Happiness comes from our sense of not being separate from one another or from nature. Happiness comes from our sense of connectedness to each other and to nature.

Laugh and the world laughs with **you**.

Ella Wheeler Wilcox

It's always too
early to quit.

Norman Vincent Peale

HOME SWEET HOME

Love the place you live. Sometimes being away from home reminds us of how fond of it we really are. Look with renewed eyes on your home and appreciate everything your area has to offer. Try being a tourist in your home town – you may make some interesting discoveries!

True happiness comes
from the joy of deeds
well done, the zest of
creating things new.

Antoine de Saint-Exupéry

If you want your life to be a magnificent story, then begin by realising that you are the author.

Mark Houlahan

YOU ARE NOT YOUR EMOTIONS

When a strong emotion arises – such as anger, hurt or fear – allow yourself to pause before you react. Notice your breath and the sensations in your body. You may then recognise that you have a choice about what you do next.

BE HAPPY. IT'S ONE WAY OF BEING WISE.

Colette

Happiness is when
what you think, what
you say and what you
do are in harmony.

Mahatma Gandhi

IT'S A VISION THING

Create a 'vision board' collage which depicts what goals and priorities you want to fulfil in your life. Keep your vision board in view so that you can frequently look at it and remind yourself of the happy direction your life is taking.

Keep your best wishes
close to your heart and
watch what happens.

Tony DeLiso

May you live every
day of your life.

Jonathan Swift

OLDER AND WISER

As we get older we grow happier. With maturing years we better appreciate the true value of family and friends, which makes us feel more content. Our brains also contain increased levels of the chemicals that enable us to feel stable and sanguine. Let's raise a toast to our elder years!

The important thing…
is not how **many** years
in your life, but how
much **life** in your years!

Edward Stieglitz

Happiness is not a
state to arrive at, but a
manner of travelling.

Margaret Lee Runbeck

The more light you
allow within you, the
brighter the world
you live in will be.

Shakti Gawain

A COMFORTABLE NEST TO COME HOME TO

If you are redecorating your home, consider the best colours that elicit a happy response for you. Everyone has different tastes, so choose colours that are calming, yet uplifting. As a result you will feel more positive about returning home to your joyful surroundings.

TO SUCCEED IN LIFE, YOU NEED THREE THINGS: A WISHBONE, A BACKBONE AND A FUNNY BONE.

Reba McEntire

Happiness consists not in having much, but in being content with little.

Marguerite Gardiner

SPREAD A LITTLE HAPPINESS

It really is true – by helping others, we feel happier. It's a great exchange for a little bit of your time each week. Check out your local charities to see how you can get involved and volunteer.

If you have a garden
and a library, you have
everything you need.

Cicero

Look at everything
as though you were
seeing it for the
first or last time.

Betty Smith

THINK POSITIVE

If you experience the noise of negative chatter in your mind, remember that it is a sign you need to attune to a positive, happier state. You have the capacity to do this by sitting still and listening to the inner wisdom that resides within you. Don't buy into the myth of your inadequacy.

It is **never** too
late to be what you
might have been.

George Eliot

The foolish man
seeks happiness in
the distance, the wise
grows it under his feet.

James Oppenheim

If you want to
be happy, be.

Leo Tolstoy

SWITCH OFF AND TUNE IN

Take time to unplug from technology. If you're waiting in a queue, resist the urge to check texts and emails on your phone. Take notice of your posture and adjust it to be comfortable. Focus on your breathing while you wait, remaining calm and undisturbed.

LAUGHTER IS THE SOUND OF THE SOUL DANCING.

Jarod Kintz

Whoever is happy will
make others happy too.

Anne Frank

What soap is to
the body, laughter
is to the soul.

Yiddish proverb

CHOOSE WISELY AND FOLLOW YOUR HEART

It is said in Native American lore that there are two wolves within your heart. You can feed the wolf of love and happiness or the wolf of hate and ill will – whichever one you feed will grow.

Be **content** with what you have; rejoice in the way things are. When you **realise** there is nothing lacking, the whole world belongs to you.

Lao Tzu

A table, a chair, a bowl of fruit and a violin; what else does a man need to be happy?

Albert Einstein

INSPIRE YOURSELF EVERY DAY

Do you find yourself thinking things like, 'I'm not clever enough' or 'I'm never going to be good at this'? If so, it's time to press the delete button on negative self-talk and replace it with something more positive. Write down some inspiring phrases and read them to yourself daily.

All life is an experiment.
The more experiments
you make, the better.

Ralph Waldo Emerson

Moderation. Small helpings. Sample a little bit of everything. These are the secrets of happiness and good health.

Julia Child

BUILD AN INSPIRATIONAL LIBRARY

Keep some of your favourite pieces of writing close to hand, so that you can refer to them when you feel yourself slipping towards negativity. Poems, prayers, song lyrics or phrases from a favourite novel can all replenish and inspire.

IT IS ALWAYS THE SIMPLE THAT PRODUCES THE MARVELLOUS.

Amelia Barr

It's never too late to have
a happy childhood.

Wayne Dyer

GIVE CBT A CHANCE

If you find yourself worrying excessively about things, it may be worth trying some cognitive behavioural therapy (CBT). This is a brief, one-to-one treatment to help you notice when you are worrying, break the habit and then implement alternative ways of reacting to your everyday problems.

Those who bring
sunshine into the lives
of others cannot keep
it from themselves.

J. M. Barrie

Every day brings a
chance for you to draw
in a breath, kick off
your shoes... and dance.

Oprah Winfrey

SMILE INSIDE

Try an internal smile – think of something happy and wonderful and experience the warm smiling feeling within. You can tap into this internal smile whenever you wish. This technique will provide you with comfort when you're feeling low, and when you're feeling fine it will simply give you a lovely boost!

Don't save things for
a **special** occasion.
Every day of your life is
a special **occasion**.

Anonymous

Every moment is a
fresh beginning.

T. S. Eliot

DOING IS BETTER THAN HAVING

Spending your money on 'experiences' – like eating out and travelling to new or favourite places – rather than on expensive items can be very rewarding. Research indicates we glean more happiness from our memories than from material things, so consider this next time you reach for your purse or wallet.

Angels can fly
because they take
themselves lightly.

G. K. Chesterton

It's never too late
– never too late to
start over, never too
late to be happy.

Jane Fonda

TRANSMIT YOUR HAPPY THOUGHTS

Share your own happiness by sending joyful thoughts to someone who is feeling sad or unwell. Simply bring them to mind and imagine you are directing loving wishes towards them, to arrive even faster than special delivery.

LIFE ISN'T ABOUT WAITING FOR THE STORM TO PASS; IT'S ABOUT LEARNING TO DANCE IN THE RAIN.

Anonymous

What we see depends
mainly on what
we look for.

John Lubbock

ALLOW YOURSELF TO BE A CHILD AGAIN

Do you remember how things seemed magical when you were a child? Look out for moments of enchantment, courtesy of nature: a rainbow, shimmering raindrops on tree branches or birdsong. Allow yourself to cherish these glimpses of wonder in your heart.

Be yourself; everyone
else is already taken.

Oscar Wilde

Laughter is a sunbeam
of the soul.

Thomas Mann

WRITE DOWN YOUR GOALS

Create an 'action list'. Place on it things you have been meaning to try, future goals for your work and ideas for spending time with friends and family. Look over it now and again to remind you of life's possibilities and to nudge you into new directions.

Life is a **helluva** lot more fun if you say 'yes' rather than 'no'.

Richard Branson

You will never be
happier than you
expect. To change your
happiness, change
your expectation.

Bette Davis

CELEBRATE WHENEVER YOU CAN!

There are many opportunities, outside of birthdays, to share happiness and gratitude: the completion of a big work project, the all-clear with a health issue, the start of something new. All of life's stepping stones deserve joyful acknowledgement.

You have to be
willing to get happy
about nothing.

Andy Warhol

Love is the
energy of life.

Robert Browning

TAKE TIME TO MAKE OTHER PEOPLE HAPPY

Think about how you can create more happiness for others. Thinking and planning something special for another person can be as enjoyable and fulfilling as the recipient's experience. It could be as simple as a birthday card, or as extravagant as a surprise party!

WE'RE ALL GOLDEN SUNFLOWERS INSIDE.

Allen Ginsberg

I've always thought people would find a lot more pleasure in their routines if they burst into song at significant moments.

John Barrowman

CONSIDER A CAREER CHANGE

Many people are now choosing happiness by developing a 'lifestyle business'. This is where you work on something you are passionate about, and is location independent with flexible hours. It can be started alongside your paid job and quite often works well with child-rearing. So be creative and think outside the box to manifest the life–work balance that you really want.

The happiness of
life is made up of
minute fractions – the
little, soon forgotten
charities of a kiss or a
smile, a kind look or
heartfelt compliment.

Samuel Taylor Coleridge

Give out what you most
want to come back.

Robin Sharma

GO WITH THE FLOW

Be flexible and let go of fixed expectations. This gives you the opportunity to embrace whatever comes your way and not regret things turning out differently. *C'est la vie!*

Remember,

happiness doesn't
depend upon who you
are or what you have,
it depends solely upon
what you **think**.

Dale Carnegie

Do anything, but
let it produce joy.

Henry Miller

the little book of
POSITIVITY

lucy lane

THE LITTLE BOOK OF POSITIVITY

Lucy Lane

£5.99
Hardback
ISBN: 978-1-84953-788-9

In a world where we're constantly bombarded by work and worry, we all need a little boost to our happiness levels now and then. This book of inspiring quotations and simple, easy-to-follow tips provides you with practical advice on thinking positively and achieving a more balanced attitude to life.

If you're interested in finding out
more about our books, find us on
Facebook at **Summersdale Publishers**
and follow us on Twitter
at **@Summersdale**.

www.summersdale.com